BIGGEST NAMES IN SPORTS
ADAM THIELEN
FOOTBALL STAR

by Chrös McDougall

FOCUS READERS.
NAVIGATOR

WWW.FOCUSREADERS.COM

Copyright © 2020 by Focus Readers®, Lake Elmo, MN 55042. All rights reserved. No part of this book may be reproduced or utilized in any form or by any means without written permission from the publisher.

Focus Readers is distributed by North Star Editions:
sales@northstareditions.com | 888-417-0195

Produced for Focus Readers by Red Line Editorial.

Photographs ©: Bruce Kluckhohn/AP Images, cover, 1, 27; Winslow Townson/Panini/AP Images, 4–5; Matt Rourke/AP Images, 7; Al Tielemans/AP Images, 9; David Durochik/AP Images, 10–11; Joseph Sohm/Shutterstock Images, 13; Pat Christman/Mankato Free Press/AP Images, 15; Jim Mone/AP Images, 16–17; Bill Wippert/AP Images, 19; Rich Gabrielson/Icon Sportswire, 21; Matt Ludtke/AP Images, 22–23; Alex Brandon/AP Images, 25; Red Line Editorial, 29

Library of Congress Cataloging-in-Publication Data
Library of Congress Cataloging-in-Publication Data is available on the Library of Congress website.

ISBN
978-1-64493-056-4 (hardcover)
978-1-64493-135-6 (paperback)
978-1-64493-293-3 (ebook pdf)
978-1-64493-214-8 (hosted ebook)

Printed in the United States of America
Mankato, MN
012020

ABOUT THE AUTHOR

Chrös McDougall is an author, sportswriter, and editor from Minneapolis, Minnesota. Like Adam Thielen, he grew up imitating Vikings stars Cris Carter and Randy Moss. Unlike Thielen, he never did it very well.

TABLE OF CONTENTS

CHAPTER 1

CAN'T STOP HIM

The quarterback took the snap, and Minnesota Vikings wide receiver Adam Thielen took off running. A Philadelphia Eagles defender stayed close to him. That didn't last long. Thirteen yards into his run, Thielen stutter-stepped and faked left. Then he cut back upfield to the right.

Thielen fights for yardage during a 2018 game against the Eagles.

By the time Thielen turned back to look for the pass, he was wide open.

Vikings quarterback Kirk Cousins had already thrown the ball. Diving for the catch, Thielen reached out and wrapped his hands around the ball. It was a 24-yard reception. And Thielen was just getting started in this 2018 game.

In a second-quarter drive, Thielen made four catches. Two went for first downs. The last one scored a touchdown. Starting three yards shy of the end zone, Thielen ran a diagonal **route**. Two defenders chased him. But Thielen calmly brought in the ball just before stepping out of bounds.

Thielen hauls in a touchdown against the Eagles.

In the third quarter, Cousins dropped back into the end zone. Under pressure, he lofted a pass toward the near sideline. Thielen had outrun his defender, and he caught it in stride. Then he kept running for a 68-yard gain.

Thielen's **versatility** was on full display. He went on to catch seven passes for 116 yards. That made him the first player since the 1960s to start a season with five 100-yard receiving games in a row. But the Vikings coaches knew Thielen was reliable no matter what they asked him to do.

SUPPORTING THE COMMUNITY

Thielen was having the best season of his career in 2018. His mind was on more than football, though. That September, he and his wife Caitlin created a **foundation** to help others. Their first move was to donate $100,000 to a local children's hospital. Adam and Caitlin, who both grew up in Minnesota, said they wanted to support the local community.

Thielen tied a league record in 2018 by going eight straight games with at least 100 receiving yards.

In the fourth quarter, Thielen fielded a punt deep in Vikings territory. Then, with just over a minute left, he smothered an **onside kick** to secure the 23–21 win. It was just another day for one of the league's most dynamic, yet unlikely, stars.

CHAPTER 2

MINNESOTA MADE

Adam Thielen was born on August 22, 1990, in Detroit Lakes, Minnesota. Growing up, Adam loved to play sports. Football was always his favorite. He would try to imitate the moves of Cris Carter and Randy Moss. They were star receivers for the Minnesota Vikings.

Cris Carter spent 12 seasons with the Vikings from 1990 to 2001.

In high school, Adam made the **varsity** team in four sports. Basketball might have been his best sport. He set the school record for career points scored. He also played football, baseball, and golf.

Adam wanted to play sports in college. However, college coaches weren't sure

METRODOME DREAMING

In high school, Adam taped a picture to his locker. It showed the Metrodome, which was where the Vikings played. But more importantly to Adam, it was also home to the high school state tournaments. Adam was determined to play at the Metrodome. Unfortunately, his high school team never quite made it. But in 2013, Thielen finally got to play there as a member of the Vikings.

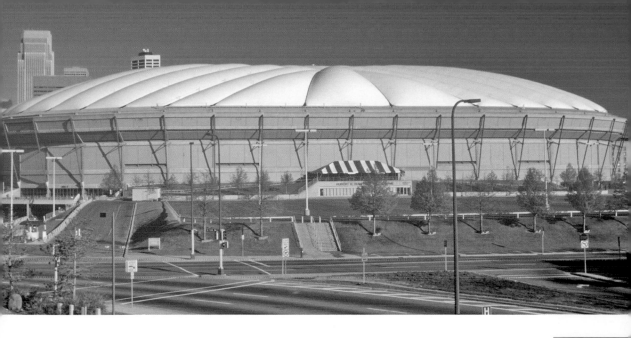

The Metrodome was the Vikings' home from 1982 to 2013.

he was big enough. Concordia College was a small school in nearby Moorhead, Minnesota. Concordia offered Adam a chance to play both basketball and football. But the summer before college, Adam met a coach from Minnesota State University. The coach offered Adam a $500 **scholarship** to play football there. Adam jumped at the opportunity.

As a college student, Thielen just wanted to keep playing football. He worked to get bigger and stronger. He also practiced staying on his feet after making a catch. That helped him gain more yards. Before long, Thielen was able to take on bigger roles with the team.

By his sophomore year, he was a standout wide receiver. He also played on **special teams**. As a senior in 2012, Thielen led the Mavericks in receiving. His play even helped the team reach the national semifinals.

After the season was over, Thielen applied for a job with a company that sold dental equipment. It was the kind

Thielen attempts to catch a pass during a college game in 2012.

of job that could lead to a good career. But Thielen wasn't quite ready to give up on sports. First, he wanted to take a shot at playing in the National Football League (NFL).

CHAPTER 3

GOING FOR IT

Players from lower-level colleges are rarely selected in the NFL **Draft**. And undrafted players rarely make it to the NFL. Both situations applied to Adam Thielen. Few NFL teams had even heard of him during his time at Minnesota State. So it was little surprise when no team picked him in the 2013 NFL Draft.

Thielen takes part in a drill during a mini-camp in the summer of 2013.

Thielen didn't give up. That spring, he had attended a small pre-draft showcase. The hometown Minnesota Vikings heard about his performance there. So they invited Thielen to a **rookie** mini-camp. Eleven other wide receivers joined him. For most of them, this was as close to the NFL as they would ever get.

The team put the players through drills. One was the 40-yard dash. No one ran it faster than Thielen. The coaches also noticed his receiving skills. Thielen ran his routes just right. The ball seemed to stick to his hands, too. At night, Thielen stayed in his room to study the playbook. He wanted to make sure he was prepared.

Thielen makes an impressive catch during a 2013 preseason game against the Buffalo Bills.

Other players came from bigger colleges. Some had even been drafted. Thielen didn't let that intimidate him.

He went all out every day. When the camp was done, the Vikings cut most of the players. But they invited Thielen back.

He still had a long way to go. The Vikings already had four good receivers. That left just one open spot. The team decided Thielen wasn't quite ready. Instead, the Vikings assigned him to the practice squad. Thielen could train with the team but not play in games. His dream lived on.

One year later, Thielen was back at training camp. This time he made the team. Fans might not have noticed him on September 7, 2014. Thielen didn't have any catches against the St. Louis

Thielen attempts to catch a pass during a 2014 game against the New England Patriots.

Rams in his first NFL game. The Vikings saw him more as a special teams player. He was asked to do a lot of the hard work that doesn't show up on the highlights. Over his first two seasons, Thielen caught just 20 passes for 281 yards. He was determined to show he could do more.

CHAPTER 4

LIVING THE DREAM

Two Green Bay Packers defenders chased Adam Thielen down the sideline. A long pass floated his way. Without slowing down, Thielen grabbed the ball and raced to the end zone. It was a 71-yard touchdown reception. Thielen ended the December 2016 game with 202 receiving yards and two touchdowns.

In 2016, Thielen became the fifth player in team history to gain 200 receiving yards in one game.

The Vikings ended up losing the game. But Thielen had finally made his mark in the NFL.

Coming into the 2016 season, Thielen was a feel-good story. He had overcome long odds to make the team he grew up cheering for. But he was a backup receiver and special teams player. Now he just had to master the little details that set the great receivers apart from the good ones.

Thielen worked on his technique in practice. He also built up his strength. That all showed in 2016. Thielen emerged as one of the league's most dangerous deep threats. He led the Vikings with 967 receiving yards.

Thielen powers past a Washington defender in 2016.

By 2017, Thielen was one of the league's best receivers. His 91 catches and 1,276 receiving yards both ranked among the top eight in the NFL. He also helped Minnesota get to within one game of the Super Bowl.

Kirk Cousins joined the Vikings in 2018. He was Thielen's fourth starting quarterback in four years. Like the other quarterbacks, Cousins quickly noticed Thielen's ability. The receiver showed a knack for getting open and being able to hold on to difficult passes.

THIELEN A PACKER?

The Green Bay Packers had three seventh-round draft picks in 2013. They considered using one on Thielen. Instead, they picked two other wide receivers. One never played for the Packers. The other had only one career catch. Thielen, meanwhile, has had some of his best games against the rival Packers.

Thielen keeps both feet in bounds as he catches a touchdown pass against the Detroit Lions in 2018.

Cousins went to Thielen often. In fact, Thielen opened the 2018 season with eight 100-yard games in a row. It was his best season yet. Thielen had shown he was more than a feel-good story. He was a true NFL superstar.

ADAM THIELEN

- Height: 6 feet 2 inches (188 cm)
- Weight: 200 pounds (91 kg)
- Birth date: August 22, 1990
- Birthplace: Detroit Lakes, Minnesota
- High school: Detroit Lakes High School (Detroit Lakes, Minnesota)
- College: Minnesota State University (Mankato, Minnesota)
- Pro team: Minnesota Vikings (2014–)
- Major awards: Second Team All-Pro (2017); Pro Bowl (2017, 2018)

Detroit Lakes

Minneapolis

Mankato

FOCUS ON
ADAM THIELEN

Write your answers on a separate piece of paper.

1. Write a paragraph describing how Adam Thielen was able to earn a spot on the Minnesota Vikings.

2. Why do you think Thielen was able to become a successful NFL wide receiver?

3. Which team considered selecting Thielen in the 2013 NFL Draft?

    A. St. Louis Rams
    B. Philadelphia Eagles
    C. Green Bay Packers

4. Why might NFL teams have passed on Thielen during the 2013 NFL Draft?

    A. They preferred to sign wide receivers as undrafted free agents.
    B. They didn't know much about Thielen because he had played at a small college.
    C. They thought he didn't work hard enough in practice.

Answer key on page 32.

GLOSSARY

draft
A system that allows teams to acquire new players coming into a league.

foundation
An organization set up by a person or group that promotes a cause, such as helping kids.

onside kick
When a football team tries to recover its own kickoff.

rookie
A professional athlete in his or her first year.

route
The path a wide receiver runs in order to get open.

scholarship
Money given to a student to pay for education expenses.

special teams
The units on a football team that play during kicking and punting situations.

varsity
The top team representing a high school or college in a sport or competition.

versatility
The ability to do a number of things well.

TO LEARN MORE

BOOKS

Frederickson, Kevin. *Wide Receivers*. Minnetonka, MN: Kaleidoscope Publishing, 2019.

Lyon, Drew. *A Superfan's Guide to Pro Football Teams*. North Mankato, MN: Capstone Press, 2018.

Whiting, Jim. *The Story of the Minnesota Vikings*. Mankato, MN: Creative Education, 2019.

NOTE TO EDUCATORS

Visit **www.focusreaders.com** to find lesson plans, activities, links, and other resources related to this title.

INDEX

Answer Key: **1.** Answers will vary; **2.** Answers will vary; **3.** C; **4.** B